Meg and Greg
The Bake Sale

Meg and Greg

The Bake Sale

with

a-e · i-e · o-e · u-e

Four Phonics Stories

Written by
Elspeth Rae and Rowena Rae

Illustrated by
Elisa Gutiérrez

ORCA two read

ORCA BOOK PUBLISHERS

Published in Canada and the United States in 2021 by Orca Book Publishers.
orcabook.com

Library and Archives Canada Cataloguing in Publication
Title: The bake sale : with four phonics stories /
written by Elspeth Rae and Rowena Rae ; illustrated by Elisa Gutiérrez.
Names: Rae, Elspeth, 1973- author. | Rae, Rowena, author. | Gutiérrez, Elisa, 1972- illustrator.
Series: Rae, Elspeth, 1973- Meg and Greg. | Orca two read.
Description: Series statement: Meg and Greg | Orca two read
Identifiers: Canadiana (print) 20210096527 | Canadiana (ebook) 20210096551 |
ISBN 9781459824966 (softcover) | ISBN 9781459824973 (PDF) | ISBN 9781459824980 (EPUB)
Subjects: LCSH: Reading—Phonetic method—Problems, exercises, etc. |
LCSH: Reading—Phonetic method— Study and teaching (Elementary) |
LCGFT: Instructional and educational works.
Classification: LCC PS8635.A39 B35 2021 | DDC jC813/.6—dc23

Library of Congress Control Number: 2021930552

Summary: This partially illustrated early chapter book, meant to be read by an advanced reader
with a beginner reader or struggling reader, combines stories and exercises that focus on phonics.

Orca Book Publishers is committed to reducing the consumption
of nonrenewable resources in the production of our books. We make
every effort to use materials that support a sustainable future.

Orca Book Publishers gratefully acknowledges the support for its publishing programs provided
by the following agencies: the Government of Canada, the Canada Council for the Arts and the
Province of British Columbia through the BC Arts Council and the Book Publishing Tax Credit.

Design and illustration by Elisa Gutiérrez

Printed and bound in Canada.

26 25 24 23 • 2 3 4 5

In this book:

a-e
and
e-e

i-e

o-e

u-e

Contents

How to read the stories in this book

Adult or buddy reader's text

Kid's text

Meg and Greg is a series of decodable phonics storybooks for children ages 6 to 9 who are struggling to learn how to read because of **dyslexia** or another language-based learning difficulty. The stories are designed for a child and an experienced reader to share the reading, as shown in the diagram above. A child feeling overwhelmed at reading sentences could start by reading only the illustration labels. More about this approach is on page 153.

What is included in these stories

The stories in this book are for a child who is familiar with all the basic **consonant** sounds (including **consonant blends**), **short vowel sounds** and the eight **phonograms** introduced in *Meg and Greg* Book 1 (*ck, sh, ch, th*) and Book 2 (*nk, ng, tch, dge*). The stories in this book focus on words that use a silent "magic" *e* to indicate that the previous vowel is pronounced with its long sound. The stories introduce words with a silent magic *e* in this order: ***a-e*** and ***e-e*** (*make, eve*), ***i-e*** (*time*), ***o-e*** (*bone*), ***u-e*** (*cute*).

The stories also use a few common words that can be tricky to sound out (see the list to the right). The child you're reading with may need help with these tricky words each time they encounter them. See pages 150–151 for more information.

Longer Words

Look out for a few words with multiple syllables. Be ready to help your child break them into individual syllables. For example, *al-pine* and *lem-on-ade*.

Words ending *se*

Also look out for words ending with the letters *se*. The *s* is often pronounced with a /z/ sound. For example, *vase, these, rise, nose, use*.

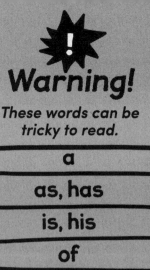

Warning!

These words can be tricky to read.

a
as, has
is, his
of
the
do, to
I
be, he, me, she, we
OK
have, give
you
"all" family (ball, small, etc.)

New for this book

what, when, where, which, why:

Five common *wh* words pronounced /w/

9

All the stories in this book introduce words that use a silent **"magic" e**. The purpose of the magic *e*, which occurs at the end of a word and stays silent (not pronounced), is to indicate that the previous vowel is pronounced with a long sound. Consider the difference between *măd* (**short vowel sound**) and *māde* (**long vowel sound**).

One way to help your child read a silent magic *e* word is this: Write a word, such as *made*, on a scrap of paper. Cross out the *e* to show that it is silent (*madé*). Next, draw an arrow to show that the silent *e* jumps backward to the previous vowel (*madé*). Last, draw a horizontal line over that previous vowel to show that it says its name (*mādé*).

Most of the time, the silent magic *e* jumps backward over only one consonant to the previous vowel. However, in a few words, it jumps backward over the blend *st* or the digraph *th*. For example, *waste, paste, bathe*.

The **silent e** has several other jobs too. These are described on page 152.

This story focuses on **a-e** words, as in *bāke* and **e-e** words such as *thēse*. There are more **a-e** words than **e-e** words in this story, simply because very few **e-e** words exist in English. It also includes the eight **phonograms** introduced in *Meg and Greg* Book 1 (*ck, sh, ch, th*) and Book 2 (*nk, ng, tch, dge*).

For a list of **a-e** and **e-e** words, including all the ones used in this story, go to orcatworead.com.

The Bake Sale

A story featuring

a-e

and

e-e

gate

bake sale

Pete

Let's **Bake!**

steps · gate · grass

Meg opened the **gate** from her backyard and
ran to Greg's house. *Knock, knock!* Rocket
barked, and then Greg opened the door.

"Hi Greg!" Meg said. "I need your help!"

"With what, Meg?" Greg asked.

"A **bake sale**," she said. "I need to hold a
bake sale right now. This instant!"

"Are you all right, Meg?" Greg asked.

Meg took a deep breath. "I saw a pretty locket at **Gabe's** Gift Store this morning. I want to get it for my mom's birthday, but I don't have enough money saved up."

"OK," Greg said. "But what's the rush? We can hold a **bake sale** on the weekend."

Meg shook her head. "My mom's birthday is tomorrow. I want to buy the locket first thing in the morning."

"I get it," Greg said.

Chapter 2

Red Velvet **Cupcakes**

Greg grabbed his lucky apron and followed
Meg. In her kitchen, Meg flung open the
cupboards while Greg looked at the recipe.

"What do we need?" Meg asked.

Greg read aloud. "Flour, cocoa, baking soda,
butter, sugar, milk, eggs and red food dye."

Meg **made** a pile of ingredients on the
counter and started looking for bowls and
the mixer.

Greg licked the wooden spoon he had used to **scrape** out the last bits of **cake** batter. Meg put the **cupcakes** in the oven. Then she looked at the clock on the wall. "They **take** twenty minutes to **bake**, so let's set up our **cupcake** and **lemonade** stand while we wait."

Greg nodded. "Good idea."

Meg and Greg carried an old desk from Meg's **basement** outside.

"I'll get the beach umbrella from my garden," Greg said. "We can put it next to the desk for some **shade**."

"Perfect!" Meg said. "I'll get paper and markers to **make** a sign."

a-e/e-e

Meg ran into the house. Greg called after her, "Check if the **cupcakes** are ready!"

In the kitchen, Meg glanced at the clock. "Oh no!" she gasped. She opened the oven door. A cloud of black smoke **came** out. She coughed and shut the door.

mitts

Greg poked his head through the doorway. "What's that smell, Meg? Is something burning?"

"Yes, our **cupcakes**!" Meg cried.

Greg dashed into the kitchen. "Quick! **Take** them out. Where are your oven mitts?"

a-e/e-e

Chapter 3

Cupcakes Take 2

Meg began to **take** out the ingredients again. "Now we don't have enough flour or sugar. We're *never* going to **make** any money."

"Come on, Meg!" Greg said. "I can get more flour and sugar from my house. It won't **take** us long to **make** the **same** recipe again."

Meg smiled reluctantly. "OK, thanks, Greg."

When Greg got back, they **made** a new batch of batter and put the **cupcakes** in the oven to **bake**.

"This time we should wait in the kitchen," Meg said. "Let's **make** the **lemonade**."

cupcake
tins

When the **cupcakes came** out of the oven, they were perfect!

Meg ran inside to get some coins. Just then the first customer **came** along.

"Welcome!" Greg said. "What would you like?"

The lady pointed at the **plate**. "I'll **take** two of those **cupcakes**."

Greg **gave** her the **cupcakes** and then picked up the jug. "And some **lemonade**?"

"Sure. How much do I owe you?" she asked.

Greg did the math in his head. "Four dollars, please."

sale

shade

Rocket

a-e/e-e

Chapter 4

The **Lemonade** Problem

Meg jumped to her feet. "Rocket! Look what you've done!"

"Meg, don't **blame** Rocket," Greg said. "He didn't mean to knock the **lemonade** over. We can **make** more."

Meg **made** a **face**. "What about my mom's jug? Now we have to **make** even *more* money to **replace** it. This **bake sale** is a disaster."

desk

grass

lemonade

a-e/e-e

As Greg pushed open the shop door, a bell rang. The shopkeeper looked up. "Hi sonny."

Greg smiled at the man. "Do you have any **lemonade**?"

"Nope. I had another kid in here yesterday. She bought every last bottle of **lemonade**."

Greg chuckled. "Do you have any **grapes**?"

The man looked puzzled. "You don't **make lemonade** from **grapes**, sonny! You need lemons. See what you can find in the fridge at the back."

Greg smiled. "OK. Thanks." He walked to the back of the shop, humming the **lemonade** song.

A small, sad lemon sat at the bottom of the fridge.

We can't **make** a jug of **lemonade** with just that small thing!

Greg **gave** the man a **wave** to thank him and left the shop.

Not a drop of **lemonade**, Rocket!

Rocket

Pant, pant!

Then what drink *can* we sell at the **bake sale**?

29

a-e/e-e

Greg started down the **lane** toward home. "Come on, Rocket. Let's walk back while we think of another plan." As they walked, a cloud went across the sun. Greg looked up at the sky. Just then a drop of rain fell on his **face** with a splat. Soon there was another, then another.

Greg shivered. "Yikes! That **came** on fast, hey, Rocket?"

Rocket wagged his tail.

a-e/e-e

Chapter 5

A Wet **Bake Sale**

"Meg! Meg!" Greg stopped to catch his breath. "The shop didn't have any **lemonade**! But this rain is a great opportunity!"

"A what?" Meg said. "You mean an opportunity to help me get this tarp up? The rain is *wrecking* our **bake sale**!"

"Well, of course I'll help you, but that's not what I'm talking about." Greg jumped up and down. "This is an opportunity to sell *hot cocoa* with the red velvet **cupcakes**!"

Meg hung her head. "I guess so. But I doubt we'll **make** any **sales** in this rain."

a-e/e-e

Soon lots of people were sheltering under the tarp.

"**These cupcakes taste** great!" said a lady with a computer **case** tucked under her arm.

An elderly man nodded. "Yes," he said, "and this hot cocoa is such a nice **change**. Most kids just have **lemonade** for **sale**!"

"Thank goodness for **these** kids!" exclaimed a young man holding a large painting. "My artwork would have been ruined in this rain."

"Yes. They really did **save** the day!" agreed the elderly man.

After supper that evening, Meg carried the coin box from their **bake sale** to Greg's house. She dumped the money onto Greg's bedroom floor.

"Wow! How much do you think we **made**?" Meg asked.

Greg looked at the money. "I **estimate** thirty dollars."

"Oh, I hope so!" Meg said.

Greg thought for a moment. "That would **make** eighteen dollars for the locket and twelve dollars to buy your mom a new jug."

They sorted the money into piles and began counting.

a-e/e-e

The End

Turn the page
for more practice
with **a-e** words!

a-e
spelling

Spell each **a-e** word below the picture.
One letter fits into each box.

a-e
word ladder

Climb down the ladder by solving the clues and changing just one letter from the previous **a-e** word. You'll know you've done it right if the word at the bottom of the ladder matches the one at the top.

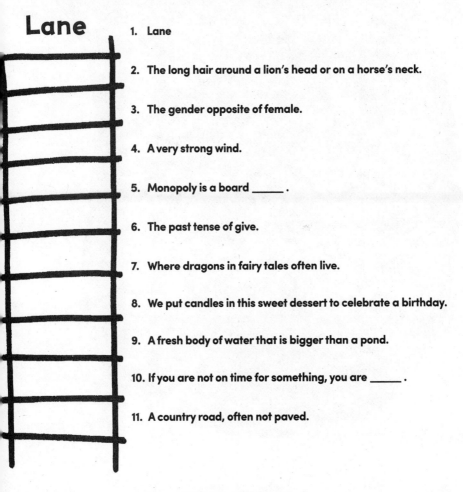

Lane

1. Lane

2. The long hair around a lion's head or on a horse's neck.

3. The gender opposite of female.

4. A very strong wind.

5. Monopoly is a board _____ .

6. The past tense of give.

7. Where dragons in fairy tales often live.

8. We put candles in this sweet dessert to celebrate a birthday.

9. A fresh body of water that is bigger than a pond.

10. If you are not on time for something, you are _____ .

11. A country road, often not paved.

Also available at orcatworead.com

All the stories in this book introduce words that use a silent **"magic"** *e*. The purpose of the magic *e*, which occurs at the end of a word and stays silent (not pronounced), is to indicate that the previous vowel is pronounced with a long sound. Consider the difference between *pĭn* (**short vowel sound**) and *pīne* (**long vowel sound**). One way to help your child read a silent magic *e* word is this: Write a word, such as *pine*, on a scrap of paper. Cross out the *e* to show that it is silent (*pin̸e*). Next, draw an arrow to show that the silent *e* jumps backward to the previous vowel (*pin̸e*). Last, draw a horizontal line over that previous vowel to show that it says its name (*pin̸e*).

The **silent e** has several other jobs too. These are described on page 152.

This story focuses on *i-e* words, as in *tīme* and *hīde*. It also includes *a-e* and *e-e* words for continued practice, as well as the eight **phonograms** introduced in *Meg and Greg* Book 1 (*ck, sh, ch, th*) and Book 2 (*nk, ng, tch, dge*).

For a list of *i-e* words, including all the ones used in this story, go to orcatworead.com.

The Bike Ride

A story featuring

smile

bike

pile

Chapter 1

Let's **Bike**

Meg picked up a bag of tiny **limes** from the shopping basket. "Why are we buying so many **limes**, Mom?"

"I'm going to make mini key **lime** pies," her mom replied.

"Yum!"

Meg's mom laughed. "Not for us. I'm helping Greg's mom. She's having the end-of-year show at her ballet studio this afternoon. The pies will be treats for all the kids and parents afterward."

Meg smiled. "Do you remember when I danced at her studio? I was a flamingo. I loved that pink costume!"

Chime!

When Meg arrived at Greg's house, his mom was getting in her car. "Hi Meg! Could you help Greg do a job for me before you go to fly his new **kite**?"

Meg nodded.

"A water **pipe** burst at my ballet studio," Greg's mom said.

Meg's eyes opened **wide**. "Oh no! What about your big show?"

"I found a new place for the show," Greg's mom said. "It just has one problem. I need to get going, but Greg will explain."

Meg turned toward Greg. "What is it?"

"The new place doesn't have changing rooms," Greg said. "So we have to deliver all the costumes to the kids. That way they can change into their costumes at home."

big **pile**

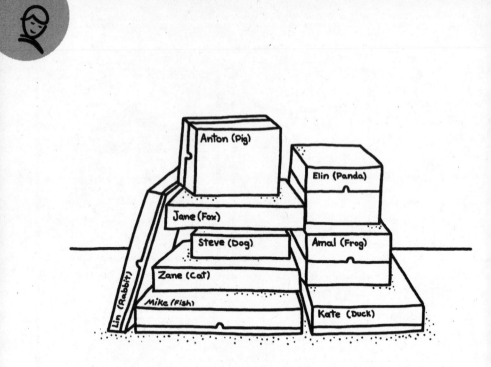

Meg frowned. "Do we have to deliver all **nine** of these boxes to different houses?"

Greg nodded. "Yup. Each kid has a different costume."

"How much **time** do we have?" Meg asked. "When does the show start?"

"This afternoon at one o'clock," Greg said.

Chapter 2

A Long **Ride**

Meg crouched to read the writing on the costume boxes. "The labels only have names. Do you know where all these kids live?"

"My mom left us a list of addresses and this map," Greg said.

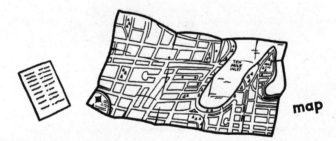

map

Meg nodded. "Great. I hope they all live **quite** close by."

"I hope so too," Greg said. "Then we will have more **time** to go **kite** flying before the show starts."

Meg raised her eyebrows. "I doubt it, but we can try."

"Who's next?" Meg asked.

"**Mike** lives at 573 Stone Avenue. So does Kate. I think they're brother and sister."

Meg frowned. "I don't know where that is. Read me the next one."

"Zane lives on **Sunrise** Ridge," Greg said. "And last is Lin on **Pine** Street."

Meg scratched her head. "I can't find any of those streets."

Greg reached across the map.

"There's **Sunrise** Ridge. And **Pine** Street too. All these kids live in **Mile** End!"

Meg's eyebrows shot up. "**Mile** End?"

Meg stared at Greg. "What are you talking about, Greg? We don't have a boat!"

Greg laughed. "No, Meg, I mean if it's low **tide**. We can cut across the inlet and save loads of **time**."

"Oh, yeah. That would definitely save us **time**," Meg said.

Greg nodded. "Let me check the **tide** table." He studied his phone. "Low **tide** is at eleven thirty. That's perfect!"

"OK, that should work," Meg said. "We can deliver the **five** near us first and then push our **bikes** across the sand." Meg jumped up. "I'll go grab my **bike**!"

Chapter 3

Rocket and the Wagon

Meg could fit only one box in her **bike** basket. Greg got three in his backpack.

"Hmm." Greg scratched his head. "How can we carry the other **five** boxes?"

"What about your red wagon?" Meg asked. "Could we pull it behind one of our **bikes** as we **ride**?"

Greg's eyes lit up. "Yes! And we don't have to pull it. Remember at Halloween last year? I made Rocket a harness to pull the wagon with all my candy!"

Rocket

Meg clapped. "That will be perfect! The wagon is just the right **size**."

Meg and Greg buckled their helmets.

"What's our first stop, Meg?" Greg asked as he climbed on his **bike**.

Meg glanced at the map. "Jane's house on **Vine** Lane."

The kids and Rocket rode in a **line** down the street.

"How's Rocket?" Meg shouted back to Greg.

Greg looked over his shoulder. "Doing just **fine**," he called. "Good boy, Rocket!"

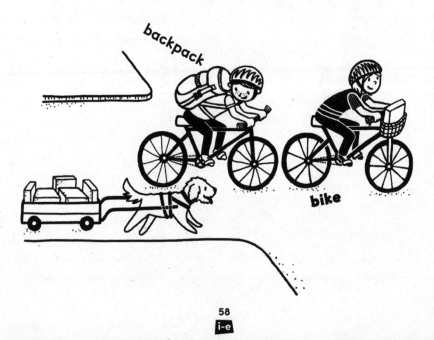

backpack

bike

i-e

Meg, Greg and Rocket set off again. After two blocks, they came to **Dime** Park.

"Let's cut across here." Greg hopped the curb and steered his **bike** onto the grass. "**Dime Drive** is on the other **side** of those trees."

Rocket

grass

Meg followed Greg, and Rocket trotted after Meg.

log

bike

Ruff! Ruff!

Bump!

Bang! Crash!

Greg sprang off his **bike** and ran to Rocket.

Rocket, you brave dog! Let me **slide** this off you.

Ruff.

Is Rocket OK?

Yes, Rocket's **fine**.

But what a mess!

Chapter 4

To **Mile** End

Meg and Greg stared at the **pile** of costumes on the grass.

"We'd better clean this up quickly," Meg said. "It's almost eleven o'clock."

Meg and Greg began stuffing the costumes back into the boxes.

red wagon

box

bikes

The woman turned to her son. "Don't take things out of the boxes, sweetie."

The little boy took his mother's hand. "Can we go play on the **slide**, Mommy?"

"Yes, let's go," the woman said. "Good luck, kids!"

Meg put the lids on the boxes and stacked them on the wagon, **while** Greg got Rocket back into the harness.

"Let's **bike** on the road this **time**," Greg said.

From Yates Street, Meg and Greg **biked** to the edge of Ten **Mile** Inlet.

Greg whooped. "Yes! It's a really low **tide**!"

Meg and Greg pushed their **bikes** onto the sand. Rocket followed them.

"This is easy!" Greg said. "We'll reach **Mile** End in no **time**."

Meg gazed into the distance. "Listen to that flock of seagulls."

Rocket barked. Greg turned to see Rocket chasing the gulls. The wagon bounced along behind him. "Rocket! Not that way! Hold my **bike**, Meg." Greg ran after Rocket, who soon slowed down. Greg caught up to him and groaned.

Chapter 5

Stuck in the **Slime**

spade

slime

Greg spotted three kids digging for clams and ran over to them. "Excuse me . . ." He stopped to catch his breath. "Could we borrow your spade? My dog and wagon are stuck back there in the **slime**."

"OK!" one of the boys replied. "I can dig them out for you. That sounds fun!"

They all splashed back through the **slime** to Rocket and the wagon. Meg had moved most of the boxes out of the wagon and put them in a **pile** by the **bikes**.

Greg took the spade and started digging. Meg and Rocket tugged at the wagon. Finally, with a loud sucking sound, the wagon came free! Everyone cheered.

"Thanks so much, kids," Greg said. "We're in a hurry to deliver those boxes, so we don't have **time** to give you a wagon **ride** today."

Meg nodded. "But we can come back tomorrow. Will you be here?"

The eldest of the three kids nodded. "Yes, we play here every day."

"Great!" Meg said. "We can fly our **kites** too."

Meg and Greg waved as they led Rocket back to the firm sand. Eventually they reached the other **side** of the inlet.

"We did it!" Greg said. "We delivered all the costumes!"

"Perfect timing too. The show starts in twenty minutes," Meg said.

"Great. Let's **ride** straight there." Greg grinned. "I'm hungry, and my mom always has food at these shows."

"Oh yeah!" Meg said. "My mom was baking mini key **lime** pies."

When Meg, Greg and Rocket arrived, Greg's mother greeted them with a big **smile**. "Well done, kids. You delivered all the costumes!"

bike

Today!

i-e

The End

Turn the page for more practice with *i-e* words!

i-e
crossword

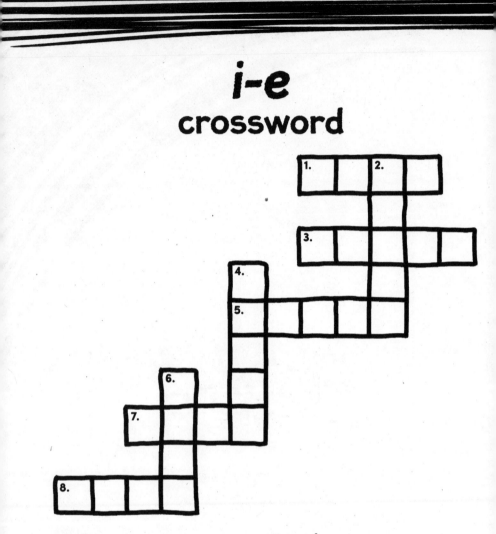

Across ➡

1. Little children love playing _____ and seek.

3. When you are happy, the corners of your mouth turn up into a _____.

5. The winner of a competition gets first _____.

7. Clocks tell us the _____.

8. Where honeybees live.

Down ⬇

2. When you get in a car, you _____ to get where you are going.

4. The bones that run along your back are also called your _____.

6. A citrus fruit similar to a lemon, but green.

Also available at orcatworead.com

i-e
match-up

Draw a line from each **i-e** or short **i** word to the correct picture.

chick

pin

nine

pipe

kite

pig

bike

All the stories in this book introduce words that use a silent **"magic" e**. The purpose of the magic e, which occurs at the end of a word and stays silent (not pronounced), is to indicate that the previous vowel is pronounced with a long sound. Consider the difference between *rŏb* (**short vowel sound**) and *rōbe* (**long vowel sound**).

One way to help your child read a silent magic e word is this: Write a word, such as *robe*, on a scrap of paper. Cross out the e to show that it is silent (*robe̸*). Next, draw an arrow to show that the silent e jumps backward to the previous vowel (*rŏbe̸*). Last, draw a horizontal line over that previous vowel to show that it says its name (*rōbe̸*). Most of the time, the silent magic e jumps backward over only one consonant to find the previous vowel. However, in one **o-e** word—*clothe*—the e jumps backward over the digraph *th*.

The **silent e** has several other jobs too. These are described on page 152.

This story focuses on **o-e** words, as in *cōde* and *hōme*. It also includes **a-e**, **e-e** and **i-e** words for continued practice, as well as the eight **phonograms** introduced in *Meg and Greg* Book 1 (*ck, sh, ch, th*) and Book 2 (*nk, ng, tch, dge*). For a list of **o-e** words, including all the ones used in this story, go to orcatworead.com.

Limestone Cove

A story featuring

slope

stones

Smoke

Chapter 1

Smoke and Pip

game

Greg was sitting on his bedroom floor, wrapped in his **bathrobe** and reading a book about the South **Pole**. His mom called up the stairs. "Greg, Mr. **Jones** is on the **phone**. He's wondering if you could take **Smoke** and Pip for a walk this morning and then take them to the dog groomer. He's offering to pay you."

Greg called back. "Sure!"

"He can be there in ten minutes, Mr. **Jones**," Greg's mom said into the **phone**.

Greg jumped up and ran downstairs. "Could I ask Meg to come too?"

His mom nodded. "Yes, of course."

path

Greg got dressed and walked over to Meg's house. "Mr. **Jones** wants me to take his dogs for a walk. Then I have to take them to the groomer at **Wishbone** Dog Shop. Do you want to come with me?"

Meg turned to her mother. "Mom, can I?"

Meg's mom smiled. "Sure. Mr. **Jones** must be holding another garden party this afternoon. He always likes Pip and **Smoke** to look fancy."

Meg and Greg set off to pick up **Smoke** and Pip.

cone

Why is that **cone** on Rocket?

He has a cut on his leg and licks it all the time. The **cone** stops him.

I can tell he hates it. I **hope** he still has fun with **Smoke** and Pip!

When Greg and Meg arrived, Mr. **Jones** was clipping a **rose** bush beside his front door. "Good morning, Greg. So kind of you to help me out. And you too, Meg."

Greg smiled. "No problem, Mr. **Jones**. What time is the appointment at **Wishbone** Dog Shop?"

"Not until noon," Mr. **Jones** replied. "So please take the dogs for a nice walk first. Perhaps let them run along the cliffs at the top of **Limestone Cove** Park?"

Greg nodded. "Great. Rocket likes running there too!"

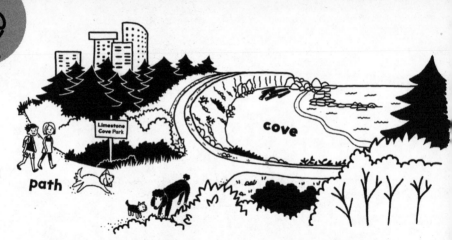

When Meg and Greg got to **Limestone Cove** Park, they unclipped the dogs' leashes. Rocket, Pip and **Smoke** ran in circles around Meg and Greg.

Greg laughed as Rocket thundered past. "That **cone** isn't slowing you down, Rocket!"

"Look at that rabbit over there," Meg said, pointing.

Smoke barked and ran toward the rabbit. Rocket and Pip followed.

Greg shouted, "Rocket, stop! Pip, **Smoke**, come back!"

As the dogs got **close** to the edge of the cliff, the rabbit vanished down its **hole**. The dogs disappeared from sight!

Chapter 2

A Big **Joke**

"Rocket! Come!" Greg called. Rocket wasn't listening. In the **cove** at the bottom of the **slope**, the three dogs were running around having fun.

"Pip, stay out of the sun," Meg shouted down.

Greg laughed. "You think she understands you, Meg?"

Meg laughed too. "Maybe not. But Mr. **Jones** did say Pip could get **sunstroke!**"

Greg called down to the **cove** again. "Rocket! Come here!"

Rocket ran in the opposite direction.

Meg stood with her hands on her hips. "They'll never come back up on their own. I think we'll have to go down to fetch them."

Greg looked along the cliff, searching for an easy way to get to the **cove**. "I can't see any steps or even a path going down the **slope**."

Meg frowned. "Neither can I."

logs

cove

rocks

o-e

The **slope** had lots of small, slippery **stones**. Meg started sliding on her feet but soon ended up on her backside! Greg grabbed an old **rope** attached to a tree branch and slid partway down the **slope** before the **rope** snapped, landing him on his backside too.

At the bottom of the **slope**, the dogs raced over, barking happily.

"Ruff!"

"Yip!"

"Yap!"

Meg and Greg laughed.

stones

slope

rope

o-e

Chapter 3

Stuck in the **Cove**

rocks

Meg climbed up onto the rocks. "Maybe we can get around to the next **cove**."

Greg shook his head. "Not with the dogs, Meg. It will be too dangerous. Let's go back to where we slid down."

As Meg and Greg walked along the sand, they threw sticks into the water for **Smoke** to fetch. Pip trailed behind, sniffing at crab **holes**. Greg had Rocket on his leash, so he wouldn't run into the water with the **cone** on his head.

Greg and Rocket went to look for the best way to get back up the **slope**.

Meg stayed with **Smoke** and Pip and threw sticks for them. **Smoke dove** into the water again and again. Pip swam back and forth with just her **nose** out of the water.

Meg threw another stick. **Smoke** got to it first. Instead of turning back, Pip swam into deeper water.

"Stay **close**," Meg called to Pip.

logs

stones

rocks

o-e

Greg ran back to Meg and tossed her the **rope**. "What are you going to do with it?"

Meg pointed up the beach. "We can tie the **rope** around that log at the bottom of the **slope** and pull it into the water. If we can float the log out to Pip and get her to jump on, we can use the **rope** to tow her back in."

Greg nodded. "OK. I **hope** it works."

Together Meg and Greg dragged the log over the **stones** and into the water. Meg tied the **rope** to one end, and Greg pushed the log toward Pip.

Chapter 4

Pip Gets a **Ride**

rope

cone

Smoke

log

Meg scratched Pip's ears. "Pip, you scared us! Thank goodness you're OK!"

Pip yipped and rolled happily in the sand. **Smoke** joined in.

Greg laughed. "Time to get to **Wishbone** Dog Shop! You dogs are a mess!"

Meg and Greg slid back down to the beach.
"Here, Pip. You can ride in my backpack."

Meg grinned. "Lucky Pip!"

"We can each help one of the big dogs,"
Greg said.

Greg helped Rocket, and Meg helped
Smoke. With lots of pushing and a little bit of
slipping, they finally left the **cove** behind.

Meg pointed to a spot near the top of the
cliff. "Look! The rabbit is watching us again."

slope

Smoke ran the last bit.

The rabbit shot back in its **hole** as **Smoke** got **close**.

hole

We did it!

path

Meg, Greg, Rocket and **Smoke** set off to **Wishbone** Dog Shop. Pip **rode** in Greg's backpack.

Chapter 5

Wishbone Dog Shop

Meg, Greg and the dogs left **Limestone Cove** Park and **wove** through busy streets to **Wishbone** Dog Shop. They walked through the door at twelve thirty.

"You're half an hour late," the groomer said. "I'm sorry, but we will have to **postpone** the appointment until tomorrow. I'm busy with other dogs now."

Greg groaned. "We lost track of the time! What are we going to do? Mr. **Jones** is having his garden party today."

Meg frowned. "And Pip and **Smoke** are filthy!"

Suddenly Meg clapped her hands. "I know what to do!" she said. "We can give them a bath and groom them at **home** ourselves."

Back at **home**, Meg gathered soap and towels. Greg picked twigs and bits of seaweed out of the dogs' fur.

"Greg, look at these cute ribbons. We can tie them in their hair," Meg said.

hose

Smoke

Greg glanced up. "It's fur, Meg, not hair."

"Same thing," Meg said. "This ribbon has little **roses** on it."

Greg brought his mom's hair dryer outside. Rocket ran and hid, but Pip and **Smoke** sat still. When they were both dry and fluffy, Meg tied the ribbon with **roses** into Pip's fur. **Smoke** got a bow tie around his neck.

Meg grinned. "You doggies look adorable!"

"It's time to go **home** for the garden party," Greg announced.

The End

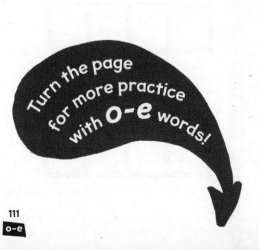

Turn the page for more practice with **o-e** words!

o-e

o-e
spelling

Spell each **o-e** word below the picture.
One letter fits into each box.

o-e
find the spelling

Put a circle around the correct spelling for each picture.

	doge	dog
	pope	pop
	note	not
	smock	smoke
	home	hom
	loge	log
	throne	thron

Also available at orcatworead.com

All the stories in this book introduce words that use a silent **"magic"** *e*, which occurs at the end of a word and stays silent (not pronounced). One way to help your child read a silent magic *e* word is this: Write a word, such as *cube*, on a scrap of paper. Cross out the *e* to show that it is silent (*cub∅*). Next, draw an arrow to show that the silent *e* jumps backward to the previous vowel (*cub∅*). Last, draw a horizontal line over that previous vowel to show that it says its name (*cūb∅*).

In the case of **u-e** words, the magic *e* indicates that the previous vowel is pronounced with either a /ū/ or an /oo/ sound. For the /ū/ sound, consider the difference between *cŭb* (**short vowel sound**) and *cūbe* (**long vowel sound**). For the /oo/ sound, consider the difference between *dŭd* (short vowel sound) and *dude* (/oo/ sound). Be ready to help your child with these two sounds as they read each **u-e** word.

The **silent e** has several other jobs too. These are described on page 152.

This story focuses on **u-e** words such as *cūte* and *flūte*. It also includes **a-e**, **e-e**, **i-e** and **o-e** words for continued practice, as well as the eight **phonograms** introduced in *Meg and Greg* Book 1 (*ck, sh, ch, th*) and Book 2 (*nk, ng, tch, dge*).

For a list of **u-e** words, including all the ones used in this story, go to orcatworead.com.

June
and the
Kittens

A story featuring

u-e

tube

jute
wine

June

Chapter 1

A Job on **Dune** Drive

Meg was helping Greg do his newspaper route.

"Greg! Guess what?" Meg said. "We've got another job—watering a garden."

"Great!" Greg said. "Whose garden?"

"A friend of my mom's," Meg said. "She's going away for three weeks with an orchestra. I think she plays the **flute**."

"Neat! Where does she live?" Greg asked.

"In Mile End, on **Dune** Drive," Meg said.

"Mile End!" Greg exclaimed. "Those houses are **huge**."

Meg laughed. "This is just a **cute** little place called **Neptune** Cottage."

Meg stopped and rummaged through her backpack. She pulled out a crumpled paper.

u-e

The next morning Meg's mom packed a picnic lunch for Meg and Greg. They were going to eat on the sand **dunes** after watering the garden on **Dune** Drive. Meg and Greg rode their bikes to **Neptune** Cottage. Rocket trotted beside them.

When they arrived, Meg looked around in wonder. "Wow! This garden *is* **huge**!" She turned on the black hose and started watering the vegetable patch.

Greg read the labels at the end of each row of vegetables. "Carrots, cabbages, pumpkins, tomatoes, **cukes** ... What's a *cuke*?"

"*Cuke* is short for *cucumber*," Meg said.

"Ruff! Ruff!"

Greg looked up. "Rocket?"

Meg glanced around the garden. "I can't see him."

Greg followed the sound of Rocket's barking to the back of the house. Rocket was growling as he stared underneath a rickety wooden deck.

"Rocket! Little buddy, what's wrong?" Greg asked.

Just then Greg heard a sound. He crouched next to Rocket and peered into the darkness. The only things he could see were old cans of paint and **tubes** of window sealant.

Rocket sprang forward as the cat hissed again.

"Rocket, don't get too close!" Greg called. He tried to grab Rocket's collar, but the dog was on his belly, wriggling toward the cat.

cans

tube

"Careful, Greg," Meg said. "This is the rotten deck. Remember **rule** 4!"

Chapter 2

The Rotten Deck

Greg ruffled Rocket's fur. "That's why the cat scratched you, Rocket. She was protecting her kittens. I should not have called her a **brute**."

Rocket woofed.

Meg got the list of instructions and **rules** from her backpack. "The lady didn't say anything about a cat. I think I should ask my mom."

Meg fetched her phone and called her mom. Greg watched the cat and kittens.

"My mom says her friend doesn't have a cat," Meg said. "For now, she thinks we should move them to a safer spot. Then she will help us decide what to do next."

Meg glanced around the garden. "I've never heard of a cat eating vegetables."

"Let's get some string," Greg said. "Maybe the cats would come out to play with it."

Meg nodded. "I'll see what's in the shed."

pot

rake

Greg called to the cats hidden behind the cans and **tubes**. "Here, kitties!"

"Hiss! Hiss!"

"Woof! Woof!"

Greg looked up just as Rocket sprang onto the deck. The dog's paws sank into the rotten wood. "Rocket, no!"

Chapter 3

Cubes of Chicken

cans

tube

The mother cat swatted at the string, but she didn't chase it.

"Come on, kitty!" Greg said. "You and your kittens will be safer in the shed."

Meg frowned. "The mother cat must be hungry. If only we had some food with us."

Greg sat up. "We do! We brought a picnic lunch, remember?"

Meg clapped. "Of course! Let's check and see what my mom packed us."

Greg smiled. "I hope it's not all **cukes** and other vegetables."

The cat jumped as the deck planks fell behind her. She ran toward the shed—and her kittens followed her!

Meg grinned. "Ha! That's a lucky **fluke**! She went exactly where we wanted."

Greg went to the shed door and peeked inside. "I can't see them. Where did they go?"

Meg peered over Greg's shoulder. "There's the mother cat. Next to that watering can."

"And look!" Greg cried. "One of the kittens is in a flowerpot!"

"How sweet is that!" Meg said.

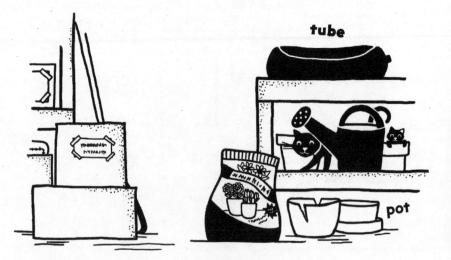

tube

pot

u-e

Meg and Greg watched from the doorway as the cat moved slowly toward the **cubes** of chicken. Her kittens followed, and soon they were all huddled in the middle of the swimming **tube**.

shelf

blanket

Greg pointed. "Look! The mother cat is wearing a collar. Maybe it has her name and phone number."

Meg held her hand out to the cat. "Can you smell chicken on my fingers?"

The cat sniffed Meg's fingers. Then she licked them and started purring.

u-e

Chapter 4

Lost Cat on **Dune** Drive

Meg gently petted the cat's head. "**June** has a collar, so she isn't a stray. She belongs to someone."

Greg nodded. "Too bad there's no phone number. How will we find her owner?"

"Let's ask next door," Meg said.

Meg, Greg and Rocket walked down **Dune** Drive to the house next to **Neptune** Cottage.

They knocked on the door, and a man answered. Meg and Greg told him about the black cat and her kittens.

"Do you know where she lives?" Meg asked.

bench

"Why do we need paper?" Meg asked.

"To make Lost Cat posters," Greg said.

While Meg and Greg wrote posters, the man fetched two bowls. "Here you go," he said. "Kibble and water for the mother cat."

Greg smiled. "Thanks!"

When they finished the posters, Meg and Greg watered the rest of the garden. Then they checked on **June**, Clove, **Jude** and **Dude** before biking to Mile End Plaza. They asked the vet, but she didn't know a black cat named **June**. She offered to put up one of their posters. Meg and Greg put up more posters at Shop and Save and the library.

That evening Meg's mom drove Meg and Greg back to **Neptune** Cottage. They ran to check on **June** and the kittens.

"They're very sweet," Meg's mom said. "I love their swimming-**tube** bed!"

Ring! Ring!

Meg's mom pulled out her phone. "I don't know this number," she said.

"Oh, Mom, I forgot to tell you!" Meg said. "We put your number on the Lost Cat posters. Maybe it's **June's** owner."

Meg's mom nodded and answered the call. "Hello?"

u-e

The next morning Meg, Greg and Meg's mom waited on the front steps of **Neptune** Cottage. Finally a car pulled up and an elderly man stepped out.

"Hello, I am Mr. **Bruce**," the man said. "I've been worried since **June** disappeared. She's been missing for nearly two weeks."

Meg smiled. "We're glad you saw our poster."

Meg's mom cleared her throat. "When we spoke on the phone yesterday, I mentioned cats..."

"**June** has kittens!" Greg blurted.

The man's eyebrows shot up. "Good gracious! Kittens?"

Chapter 5

Jude, Dude
and the Twins

The next week Meg and Greg met Mr. **Bruce** at **Neptune** Cottage every day. Together they fed and cared for **June** and played with the kittens.

"These kittens are so charming!" Mr. **Bruce** said. "They do **amuse** me."

Meg smiled. "Whoever adopts these **cute** little kitties will be very lucky."

Greg nodded. "I hope we get a call soon!"

"Look at little Clove!" Mr. **Bruce** laughed. "She's the smallest but the bravest."

Clove

Jude

Dude

u-e

Meg's mom drove to **Neptune** Cottage and found the kids and Mr. **Bruce** playing with the kittens in the sun. "We have a family coming to look at the kittens."

Meg grinned. "That's great, Mom!"

A few minutes later, a woman arrived with her sons.

"Come and meet them," Meg said to the woman.

Greg pointed at each kitten in turn. "**Jude** and **Dude** are boys. Clove is a girl."

"Mommy, they're so **cute**!" said one of the boys. "**Jude** and **Dude** are twins just like us!"

His brother hopped up and down. "Can we take them both, Mommy? Please, Mommy?"

The End

Turn the page for more practice with **u-e** words!

u-e
match-up

Draw a line from each **u-e** or short **U** word to the correct picture.

tune

cup

sun

flute

jug

cube

mute

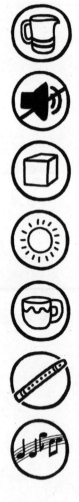

u-e
word search

Find the following **u-e** and short **U** words in the puzzle.
Words are hidden ➡ and ↓.

```
e m b c u b e h u g c v
i f l m t u b e r r u s
o l u w q f o r o u w d
t u c a t u b a n b d u
u t k b w s v m u l e g
n e q r k e i d u n e n
e c u t e e m u g a f z
y e b f n c u t d m h j
```

cube	flute	mule
cut	fuse	rub
cute	hug	tube
dug	luck	tune
dune	mug	tub

Some oddities of English explained

Do you know what's tricky about these words?

This little word can be pronounced with a **short vowel sound** (/ă/ as in *hăt*), **long vowel sound** (/ay/) or **schwa vowel sound** (/uh/).

If these words followed the standard English spelling convention, they would all end in a double *s*, as in *pass* and *kiss*. Instead, they have a single *s* and are pronounced with a /z/ sound.

Children might try to pronounce this word as /off/ instead of the pronunciations /uv/ or /ov/.

This very common word starts with the *th* letter combination (**phonogram**) and ends with a schwa-sounding vowel. The *th* phonogram is the focus of the fourth story in *Meg and Greg* Book 1.

Children might try to pronounce these words with short vowel sounds, as in /daw/ and /taw/, or even long vowel sounds, as in /doe/ and /toe/, instead of the pronunciations /doo/ and /too/.

In these words, the vowel makes a long sound.

a
as, has
is, his
of
the
do, to
I
be, he, me, she, we

Children might try to pronounce this word as /ock/ instead of reading the two individual letters.

These words look like the **magic e** words introduced in this book, but they're not. The first vowel is pronounced with a short sound, and the final e is silent. Read more about words ending with *ve* on page 152.

This word is pronounced /y-/-/oo/. Although it's fairly common for the letters *ou* to be pronounced with an /oo/ sound (*soup*, *group*), beginning readers may not be aware of this /oo/ sound for these letters, so they might need help reading it.

OK

have, give

you

"all" family (ball, small, etc.)

Words in the "all" family are pronounced /ŏ/-/l/. Beginning readers might try to pronounce the letter *a* as /ă/ as in *hăt* and so pronounce "all" as /ă/-/l/.

Five common *wh* words:

what, when, where, which, why

wh is a digraph (two letters with one sound) that in most accents is pronounced as /w/. *wh* occurs at the beginning of a word and is often used for question words, like the five introduced in this book. All of these words are difficult to sound out (not only because of the *wh* but also because of the spelling of the rest of the word). Beginning readers will likely need help reading each one of these words.

Do you know that silent *e* has many jobs?

A lot of English words end with a silent letter *e*. This **silent *e*** has many different jobs, including being a **magic *e***, which is the focus of this book. Read on for some silent *e* jobs.

1. **Magic *e***: The silent *e* indicates that the previous vowel is pronounced with a **long sound**. Examples are *made, eve, tide, home, cube*.

2. **Words ending with *ve* or *ze***: English words never end with the letter *v* or a single letter *z*. In the case of the letter *v*, a silent *e* always protects it. Examples are *have, twelve, olive, curve*. In the case of the letter *z*, the *z* is doubled (*buzz, fizz*) or a silent *e* is added to protect it (*breeze, snooze*).

3. **Words ending with *se***: The silent *e* prevents some words from inadvertently looking like a plural word. Think about the word *moose*. Without a silent *e*, the word looks like this: *moos*. But would *moos* mean one large wild animal or multiple sounds made by a milk cow? Other examples are *pleas* vs. *please*, *brows* vs. *browse*, *tens* vs. *tense*.

4. **Words ending with *ge* or *ce***: The silent *e* ensures that the letter *c* is pronounced with its soft /s/ sound and the letter *g* is pronounced with its soft /j/ sound. Examples are *fence, dance, huge, cringe*.

5. **Words ending *th* + *e***: The silent *e* ensures that the digraph *th* is pronounced with its voiced sound /<u>th</u>/ and not the unvoiced sound /th/. Consider the examples *bathe* vs. *bath* and *clothe* vs. *cloth*.

6. **Short content words**: The silent *e* is sometimes added to a short **content word** (noun, main verb, etc.) to distinguish it from a **function word** (auxiliary verb, article, preposition, etc.) that sounds the same. For example, *bye* and *by*, *fore* and *for*. In other cases, the silent *e* adds a letter to a content word, since these words are rarely less than three letters. Examples are *ewe* and *awe*.

About the
Meg and Greg stories

Who are the *Meg and Greg* stories for?

These stories are for children who are struggling to learn how to read because they have dyslexia or another language-based learning difficulty.

We wrote the stories especially for struggling readers who are ages 6 to 9 (approximately grades 2–4), which is a little older than most kids start learning to read. These slightly older learners can understand and appreciate more complex content, but they need it written at a lower reading level. You might see this concept described with the term *hi-lo*.

To make a hi-lo concept work for children at a near-beginner reading level, we designed the *Meg and Greg* stories for shared reading. A buddy reader—an adult or other confident reader—shares the reading with the child who is learning. Each story has five short chapters and is ideal for use in one-on-one or small-group reading sessions.

Aren't there already lots of books for beginning readers?

Yes, but the many leveled readers available for beginners typically don't meet the needs of children with a learning difficulty. These children benefit from learning English incrementally and without spelling exceptions or advanced spellings thrown into the mix.

The *Meg and Greg* stories introduce one letter combination (**phonogram**) or concept at a time. Each story builds on the previous ones by including words with the phonograms and concepts already introduced.

How does shared reading work?

Each story has several layers of text so that an adult or buddy reads the part of the story with more complex words and sentences, and the child reads the part of the story with carefully selected words and shorter sentences. Quite literally, *two read*.

Each story has:
- *Illustration labels* for a child just starting to read or feeling overwhelmed at reading sentences. The labels are single words or short phrases and contain the story's target letters as often as possible.

- *Kid's text* for a child who has mastered the sounds made by the basic **consonants** (including **consonant blends**), **short vowels** and the eight **phonograms** introduced in *Meg and Greg* Book 1 (*ck, sh, ch, th*) and Book 2 (*nk, ng, tch, dge*). The kid's text appears on the right-hand page when the book is open to a story. We also used kid's text for all story and chapter titles. As we created the stories, we bound ourselves to a set of rules that controlled the words we were "allowed" to use in the kid's text. If you're interested in these rules, they are listed on our website (orcatworead.com).

- *Adult or buddy reader's text* is the most difficult, and it always appears on the left-hand page when the book is open to a story. The buddy text uses longer sentences, a wider vocabulary and some letter combinations that the beginning reader has likely not yet learned, but it avoids very difficult words.

A child who is a more advanced reader and simply needs practice with the target letter combination can try reading all three layers of text in the story.

Are there any tips for buddy readers?

Yes! Try these ideas to help the child you're reading with:
- Keep the list of tricky words handy for the child to refer to when reading (see the lists on pages 150–151). Also be patient: the child may need help each time they encounter a tricky word, even if they only just read the word on the previous page.
- Before starting a story, have the child read the story title and each chapter title (in the table of contents). Ask them to predict what the story might be about.
- Before starting a story, write down a list of all the words the child might not be familiar with and review them together.
- Before you read a page of buddy text, have the child point out all the words with the target letter combination on the left-hand page of the open book.
- After reading each chapter, have the child speak or write one sentence that uses some of the words from the chapter. Some children might like to draw a picture.

Do the stories use "dyslexia-friendly" features?

Yes. As well as the language features throughout the story, we used design features that some people find helpful for reading:
- The font mimics as closely as possible the shapes of hand-printed letters. Children begin by learning to print letters, so we think it is important for the letter shapes to be familiar. For example, a child learns to print a not *a* and g not *g*.
- The illustration labels are printed in lowercase letters as much as possible because children often learn to recognize and write the lowercase alphabet first. A beginning reader may be less familiar with the uppercase letter shapes.
- The spaces between lines of text and between certain letters are larger than you might see in other books.
- The kid's text is printed on shaded paper to reduce the contrast between text and paper.

Glossary

a-e: Represents the **long vowel sound** /ā/ created by a silent **magic e**. *a-e* words are introduced in the first story in this book. Examples are *cake, blame, safe, waste*.

Consonant: Any letter in the alphabet except for the vowels (*a, e, i, o, u*).

Consonant blend: Two or three consonants appearing at the beginning or end of a syllable. Each consonant sound is pronounced, but the sounds are so close, they seem to be blended or "glued" together. For example, *flop, camp and sprint*.

Content word: A word that carries meaning, such as an adjective (*shaggy*), noun (*moose*), verb (*galloped*) or adverb (*clumsily*). Compare with **function word**.

Dyslexia: A term made up of *dys*, meaning "difficult," and *lexis*, meaning "word." Dyslexia tends to be used as a catchall term that describes a range of language-learning difficulties. These can include reading (fluency and comprehension), spelling, writing, organization skills (executive function) and even some aspects of speech.

e-e: Represents the **long vowel sound** /ē/ created by a silent **magic e**. *e-e* words are introduced in the first story in this book. Examples are *eve, theme, these*.

i-e: Represents the **long vowel sound** /ī/ created by a silent **magic e**. *i-e* words are introduced in the second story in this book. Examples are *pine, time, bike, swipe*.

Function word: A word that attaches content words to one another in a sentence. Examples are an auxiliary verb (*is, can*), article (*a, the*), conjunction (*and, but*), preposition (*to, by*) and pronoun (*she, him, it*). Compare with **content word**.

Long vowel sound: The way in English that a vowel sounds when we pronounce it for a long time (longer than we do **short vowel sounds**) in regular speech. Long vowel sounds are often represented by a silent **magic e**, a combination of vowels or a single vowel ocurring at the end of a syllable. For example, *bīke, mūte, rāin, trēe* and *gō*. The horizontal line, called a macron, shows that the vowel is pronounced with a long sound. Compare with short vowel sound.

Magic e: A silent (not pronounced) letter *e* at the end of a word to indicate that the previous vowel is pronounced with a long sound. Consider the difference between *măd* (short vowel sound) and *māde* (long vowel sound). **Magic e words** are the focus of this book.

o-e: Represents the **long vowel sound** /ō/ created by a silent **magic e**. **o-e** words are introduced in the third story in this book. Examples are *mōle, hōpe, stōne, thōse*.

Phonogram: Any letter or combination of letters that represents one sound. For example, the sound /k/ can be spelled with five different phonograms: c (*cat*), k (*kite*), ck (*stick*), ch (*echo*) and que (*antique*).

Schwa vowel sound: The way in English that we often pronounce the vowel in an unstressed syllable, like the *a* in *yoga*.

Short vowel sound: The way in English that a vowel sounds when we pronounce it for a short time in regular speech. For example, *ăt, nĕt, pĭg, tŏp* and *ŭp*.

Silent e: An unpronounced letter *e*. There are many jobs for a silent *e*, as described on page 152. This book focuses on silent **magic e words**.

u-e: Represents the **long vowel sound** /ū/ created by a silent **magic e**. **u-e** words are introduced in the fourth story in this book. Examples are *cūte, fūme, pūke*. Words with **u-e** can also be pronounced with an /oo/ sound, as in *Jūne, flūte, rūle*.

About the authors and illustrator

Who are the authors?

Elspeth and Rowena are sisters who believe in a world where all children learn to read with confidence *and* have the chance to discover the pleasure of being lost in a good book.

Elspeth is a teacher certified in using the Orton Gillingham approach to teach children with dyslexia and other language-based learning difficulties. She lives with her husband and three children in Vancouver, British Columbia.

Rowena is a children's writer and editor living with her two children in Victoria, British Columbia.

Elspeth

Rowena

Who is the illustrator?

Elisa is an award-winning children's book designer, illustrator and author with a passion for language and literacy. Originally from Mexico City, she lives with her husband and two children in Vancouver, British Columbia.

Elisa

Acknowledgments

We have many people to thank for helping us create this third book in the *Meg and Greg* series. Huge thanks to our editor, Liz Kemp, at Orca Book Publishers for shepherding us with care and enthusiasm through all the stages of preparing the book. We're also very grateful to Orca's amazing editing, design and marketing teams, and to Susan Korman, who reviewed the stories and gave us invaluable feedback. Special thanks to Julia Cross for inspiration and advice on creating the kitten illustrations in the fourth story.

We asked several families and students to test read the stories, and we thank them all for their comments and encouragement. They are Ila and Lincoln Anderson, Ivy and Sara dePol, Nora and Aimée Foreman, Izzy and Olivia Hong, Patricia Huscroft and her grandson, Elliot and Walter Jull, Roma and Marnie Jull, Zoe MacMillan, Imogen and Sebastian MacMillan-Thomas, Genevieve and Andrea Roszmann, Kira and Nancy Trudeau, and Genevieve and Madeleine Wilson. We also thank Haviva Davids Diena and her students at Say What Speech Therapy, as well as several of Elspeth's students at Blundell Elementary in the Richmond School District.

And thank you, readers, for joining Meg and Greg on their latest set of adventures. We had a lot of fun writing and illustrating these stories, and we hope you found them fun to read!